The Hoover Dam: The History and Cor
Engineering Project

By Charles River Editors

1942 picture of Hoover Dam

About Charles River Editors

Charles River Editors provides superior editing and original writing services across the digital publishing industry, with the expertise to create digital content for publishers across a vast range of subject matter. In addition to providing original digital content for third party publishers, we also republish civilization's greatest literary works, bringing them to new generations of readers via ebooks.

Sign up here to receive updates about free books as we publish them, and visit Our Kindle Author Page to browse today's free promotions and our most recently published Kindle titles.

Introduction

1904 picture of the site before the Hoover Dam

Hoover Dam

"This morning I came, I saw, and I was conquered, as everyone would be who sees for the first time this great feat of mankind…Ten years ago the place where we gathered was an unpeopled, forbidding desert. In the bottom of the gloomy canyon whose precipitous walls rose to height of more than a thousand feet, flowed a turbulent, dangerous river…The site of Boulder City was a cactus-covered waste. And the transformation wrought here in these years is a twentieth century marvel." – President Franklin D. Roosevelt, September 30, 1935

During the 1930s, at the height of the Great Depression, thousands of workers began work on the Hoover Dam, built in the Black Canyon, which had been cut by the powerful Colorado River. The Colorado River was responsible for the Grand Canyon, and by the 20th century, the idea of damming the river and creating an artificial lake was being explored for all of its potential, including hydroelectric power and irrigation. By the time the project was proposed in the 1920s, the contractors vowing to build it were facing the challenge of building the largest dam the world had ever known. As if that wasn't enough, the landscape was completely unforgiving, as described by the famous explorer John Wesley Powell generations earlier: "The landscape everywhere, away from the river, is of rock--cliffs of rock, tables of rock, plateaus of rock, terraces of rock, crags of rock--ten thousand strangely carved forms...cathedral shaped buttes, towering hundreds or thousands of feet, cliffs that cannot be scaled, and canyon walls that shrink the river into insignificance, with vast hollow domes and tall pinnacles and shafts set on the verge overhead; and all highly colored."

The engineering that went into the Hoover Dam was not just dangerous but unprecedented, to the extent that the Hoover Dam relied on building methods that had never been proven effective on such a giant scale. The project also had to employ tens of thousands of people in often dangerous working conditions, which resulted in scores of deaths. At the same time, however, the large number of men that traveled to work on the project helped turn Las Vegas, a nearby small desert town in Nevada, into Sin City.

Despite all the difficulties, the Hoover Dam was completed on time, and President Roosevelt summed up just how impressive the accomplishment was in his speech dedicating the site in 1935: "We are here to celebrate the completion of the greatest dam in the world, rising 726 feet above the bedrock of the river and altering the geography of a whole region: we are here to see the creation of the largest artificial lake in the world-115 miles long, holding enough water, for example, to cover the whole State of Connecticut to a depth of ten feet; and we are here to see nearing completion a power house which will contain the largest generators and turbines yet installed in this country, machinery that can continuously supply nearly two million horsepower of electric energy."

The Hoover Dam: The History and Construction of America's Most Famous Engineering Project chronicles the construction of America's most famous dam. Along with pictures of important people, places, and events, you will learn about the Hoover Dam like never before, in no time at all.

The Hoover Dam: The History and Construction of America's Most Famous Engineering Project

Chapter 1: A Vision in the Desert

"Boulder Dam was, first of all, a vision in the desert. ...in 1902 Arthur Powell Davis, having taken a civil engineering degree at Columbian University, and having spent several years as hydrographer with the abortive Nicaragua Canal Commission, began to make his own rich contribution to the Colorado's history. He studied the endless, mud-shwishing Gulliver sprawled across the sun-scorched wastes of the Southwest. Now it moved in perpetual twilight under precipices as terrifying as the cliffs of dream. Now it wound into remorseless sunlight between lonely rock horizons upon whose brows you half expected to see the stain of perspiration. Near the southern tip of Nevada the river entered Black Canyon. The walls of Black Canyon are considerably higher than the Woolworth Building and they diverge enough to be thoroughly baked by the sun. There is no hotter or more desolate scene on the Colorado - a turgid stream in a towering furnace of stone, a parching parody of all that the sweet word river has meant to the poets." – Excerpt from a 1933 article in *Fortune*

Since its inception, the Hoover Dam has been one of America's most controversial and powerful construction projects. In fact, its very name was controversial; the dam was originally named for Herbert Hoover, the president who initiated its construction, but it was later called the Boulder Dam when the former president fell out of favor with the American people. Of course, the Boulder Dam went back to being known as the Hoover Dam when time and history presented the much maligned president in a more positive light.

Hoover

However, before Hoover or any other president ever considered the idea, another, mostly forgotten man imagined what it could be. According to a 1933 article featured in *Fortune* magazine, "There in Black Canyon Arthur Powell Davis had his vision. For twenty succeeding years he gave his finest energies to the notion of the dam. Boulder Dam became a local and then a national issue. It involved scores of prominent Americans in disputes political, financial, and technical. But in the jagged valleys of the Colorado or in Washington or anywhere else there was no dispute about one fact: Boulder Dam was fundamentally the conception of Arthur Powell Davis; it was everlastingly based on his monumental engineering report."

Davis

A 1920s sketch of the proposed dam site and the resulting reservoir

That report was known as the Fall-Davis report, named after Davis and his co-author, then Interior Secretary Albert Fall. In their opinion, the Colorado River could be dammed up and used to generate a significant amount of electricity for the burgeoning population in the surrounding area, but they believed the federal government would have to take the lead in legislating its use since the river flowed through several states.

Fall

Davis had already proposed that the dam could be begun by blowing up the walls of Boulder Canyon and using whatever stone did not wash away to build it, and while that particular idea was not terribly popular, most agreed that some sort of dam should be built. However, the politics of the matter proved to be nearly insurmountable; according to *Fortune*, "In 1923 the wrangling got so hectic in the office of Secretary of the Interior Hubert Work that Mr. Davis resigned his positions as Director and Chief Engineer to the Reclamation Service. Gray and gentle and disillusioned, he went to California, where he worked on local aqueducts, and to Turkestan, where he was the Soviets' Chief Consulting Engineer on irrigation."

Meanwhile, others continued the fight, and by early 1930, with the country in the throes of an economic depression that only more jobs could cure, the federal government figured that thousands of men who were otherwise out of work could be sent west to southern Nevada to build a dam. Thus, on July 7, 1930, newspapers around the country received the following press release:

"The Secretary of the Interior announced today that construction of the Boulder Canyon project had commenced, immediately on the President's signature of the appropriation bill. The engineer in charge, Mr. Walker R. Young, and his assistants, were already on the ground waiting telegraphic instructions. The first day's work began the staking out of the railroad and the construction road, surveys of which have already been completed, laying out streets for the town site, and continuation of surveys for the water supply system. The order which started construction was signed by the Secretary immediately following the President's signature of the appropriation bill, and read as follows:

Order No. 436 Hon. Elwood Mead, Commissioner of Reclamation.

Sir: You are directed to commence construction on Boulder Dam today.

Respectfully, Ray Lyman Wilbur, Secretary.

The Secretary stated that the plans and specifications are being carried to completion with all possible expedition, looking to the advertising of bids and the awarding of construction contracts at the earliest possible date. Following the completion of the work begun today on the railroad, construction road, town site, and water works, the money appropriated will be used to commence construction of the cofferdams and diversion tunnels."

Wilbur also made a few public comments about the project, some of which reflected the perspective of the times but might offend modern environmental sensitivities: "The Boulder Dam will signalize our national conquest over the Great American Desert. With dollars, men, and engineering brains we will build a great natural resource. We will make new geography, and start a new era in the southwestern part of the United States. With Imperial Valley no longer menaced by floods, new hope and new financial credit will be given to one of the largest irrigation districts in the West. By increasing the water supply of Los Angeles and the surrounding cities, homes and industries are made possible for many millions of people. A great new source of power forecasts the opening of new mines and the creation of new industries in Arizona, Nevada, and California. To bring about this transformation requires a dam higher than any which the engineer has hitherto conceived or attempted to build."

Wilbur

Naturally, the project proved to be an immediate boost for the local community, as one woman recalled: "Now, Murl Emery had a ferry across the river before we ever began to build the dam, so all of the engineers that had been doing the surveying for everything knew Murl. He had the contract to take the men down the river in boats to the diversion tunnels. The diversion tunnels were being dug from both ends at the same time. That meant that there were 8 crews around the clock - - 24 crews a day - - going to those diversion tunnels, and they all went down river on the boats."

In addition to generating electricity, the main purpose of the Hoover Dam project was to generate jobs for those hit hardest by the Great Depression. In addition to workers, there would be need for an extensive support staff, including bookkeepers, grocery store workers, and even doctors and nurses. At the same time, however, Wilbur initially warned those desperate for jobs about what they were getting into if they decided to move to Nevada: "Of one thing the public should be warned and that is the unwisdom of going to the vicinity of the dam site in the expectation of getting work without ample provision to meet the emergency should this expectation fail. The dam site is located in the midst of a great desert with few inhabitants and slight opportunity for other employment than that which it may afford. Employment will develop only as contracts are let and ample notice will be given when opportunities for work present themselves."

Despite the official caveats, as one article pointed out, the Hoover Dam was as much a political triumph as it was an engineering feat: "Boulder Dam will not only be a monumental engineering work, but the laws authorizing it inaugurated the greatest scheme of rural planning yet undertaken in the West. That this scheme shall prove of the greatest possible value to the Nation, it necessitates now a study of all irrigation and power possibilities of the whole basin, and of the different States. Five hundred thousand dollars has been provided this year for studies of secondary projects in the Colorado Basin. This includes $100,000 for a study of the irrigation possibilities of Utah, Colorado, Wyoming, and New Mexico, the four States above Boulder Dam; $250,000 for surveys and preparation of plans and estimates for the Parker-Gila project in Arizona; and $150,000 for continuing the surveys and preparation of plans and estimates for the Palo Verde, Imperial, and Coachella Valleys. Altogether, these investigations will deal with the possible future reclamation of 6,000,000 acres of land, an area equal to that now irrigated in the lower Nile. Consideration must be given to a possible 6,000,000 horsepower electrical development on the river as a whole."

And what of Davis? According to the 1933 article in Fortune, "For ten years Boulder Dam proceeded without him. The money was at long last appropriated, actual blasting was begun. In California, far from these detonations, Mr. Davis' health began to fail. The Prosperity Party changed the name of the project to Hoover Dam. Mr. Davis' name, which had never had much advertisement in the first place, dropped out of memory as quickly as that of any ill and retired American. On June first of this year the first buckets of concrete were poured into the hugest mold ever conceived; the Colorado already writhed helplessly in a strait-jacket of stone and steel. At length in mid-July the forgotten Mr. Davis received his own particular New Deal. The new Administration concluded perhaps that just dues were better late than never, and Mr. Davis appointment as consulting Engineer on Boulder Dam was announced by Secretary Ickes. And at seventy-two Arthur Powell Davis returned, or was returned, to his vision. His health was too delicate to permit much actual field work in the Molochian jaws of Black Canyon. But on the Washington records he was back at what any of the boys on the canyon will be first to admit was his job."

Whatever joy Davis had at seeing his vision start to become reality, it was short lived. He died just a few months later, long before the dam was ever completed.

Chapter 2: The Six Companies

"The Boulder Canyon Project Act authorized federal appropriations not to exceed $165,000,000. They were apportioned as follows:

Dam and reservoir $70,600,000
Power development 38,200,000
All-American Canal 38,500,000
Interest during construction 17,700,000

One hundred and sixty is fair candy money, even for Washington. And particularly when forty-five states in the Union are not getting so much as a gumdrop. The sullen watchfulness of eastern, southern, northern, and mid-western Congressmen made a waste-proof spending plan imperative. Two set-ups were possible. The dam could be government built (cries of "No! No! The government will lose money!"). The dam could be built on private contract (cries of "No! No! The government will lose money!"). The problem was solved by compromise. The dam is under the direct supervision of the Washington and Denver offices of the U.S. Government's Bureau of Reclamation; actual designs of all its features are made in the Denver office. It is being built by a group of western contractors, calling themselves the Six Companies." – Excerpt from a 1933 article in *Fortune*

When the Federal government announced the scale of the project and its budget, companies from all over the country sat up and took notice. As the 1933 *Fortune* article proclaimed, "When Washington announced it had the job for somebody, a sudden low scribbling was heard in the land. This was the sound of estimating. Most of it died very quickly, as contractors realized the job was too huge even to bid on."

Not only was the job itself big, but in order to limit competition to only those companies who were likely large enough to see the dam completed, the government insisted that the winning bidder put up a $5 million completion bond that would be forfeited if they quit before the project was finished. In reality, no company in Depression-era America could afford to risk that kind of money. As the article continued, "But in San Francisco, Salt Lake City, Boise, and Portland, telephones jangled and very quickly the hard heads of Bechtel & Kaiser and MacDonald & Kahn (San Francisco), Morrison-Knudson Co. (Boise), Utah Construction Co. (Salt Lake City), and Portland's J.F. Shea and the Pacific Bridge Co. were put together. They set up a joint corporation capitalized for $8,000,000, called it the Six Companies, scribbled, estimated, and bid $48,890,995, bonded the contract for $5,000,000 in cash. They got the job."

And what a job it was. The article explained, "For their $48,890,995 the Six Companies must foot all construction bills - for dynamite, for trucks, for digging mud and dumping mud, for bosses' salaries, and for labor's wage. The Six companies do not pay for construction raw material - for the 5,500,000 barrels of cement consumed, or the 55,000 tons of steel plates and castings, or the turbines and generators in the power plant, or any of the permanent operating machinery of the dam. ... They were out of pocket $3,500,000 for preliminary work before they received a government penny. Until half the work was done they received only ninety cents on the dollar. The holdback is around $2,000,000, which they will receive at the end - like an ice-cream cone for being good. It suffices perhaps to say that during the first five months of 1933 the government paid an average monthly bill from the Six Companies of $1,513,000. Out of this the corporation must pay items such as a half-million a month payroll, $48,000 for gas and oil, $40,000 for electricity. At one time when the roads were roughest, they were spending $500 a day for truck and automobile tires. When the last bills are paid and the turbines begin to turn, the Six companies will have turned a profit estimated at $7,000,000 and upward for all their work."

One of the most daunting questions about building the dam was related not to engineering but to managing the workforce that would prove to be an integral part of its construction. Wilbur knew this and pointed out early on that the dam "is to be built in a region of intense summer heat, amid desert surroundings and where the public lands, in large part, are being surveyed for the first time. To build the dam economically and efficiently requires that special attention be given to those factors which influence the health and energy of the workers." This was a wise and necessary move, as the American desert and Badlands had already taken the lives of hundreds of men, women and children more rugged and prepared for hard living than those folks coming to work on the dam.

To make sure that all was done to prepare an environment conducive to productivity, Wilbur proposed the following plan: "A thousand men will be employed over a period of five to eight years. Many of these will have families, and this means that the town to be created near the dam site will have a population of 4,000 to 5,000 people. This town will not be a temporary construction camp. During the time that the dam is under construction, thousands of tourists will each year visit this section. When it has been completed, the lake 100 miles in length above it will draw other thousands because of its scenic beauties. Plans accordingly have been made to lay out a town which will represent the most modern ideas in town planning. The water works will be similar in character to those built at Yuma, Ariz., where the conditions of climate and water are similar to those at Boulder Dam. From the town site to the dam is about three miles. The town will be connected with the outside world by an automobile road and a railroad about 30 miles in length. ... Of the initial appropriation of $10,660,000, $2,500,000 will be used to build the railroad, $525,000 will be expended in the construction of waterworks, laying out the town, building streets, sewers, and other conveniences of the town, and in the construction of a main office building for the Government engineers and clerical staff and 25 homes for its permanent employees at the dam. ... In preparation for the project, the government built a new, planned community in the desert. Known as Boulder City, Nevada, it was connected by rail to the Union Pacific Railroad on September 17, 1930. Construction on the dam officially began less than two weeks later, on September 30."

While what Wilbur described was the ultimate goal, he knew all too well that it was not a good idea to sit on money that had already been appropriated by Congress for too long, so he made clear that it was "not necessary that construction of the tunnels to divert the river shall await the completion of these facilities of living and transportation. There is a good road from Las Vegas to the canyon. ... A temporary construction camp can be located on the river and the construction of the tunnels thereby expedited."

As a result, the community that the government first constructed was far from Wilbur's ideal. In fact, it was probably only the desperate times that compelled anyone to be willing to live there. According to Emma Godbey, who moved into "Ragtown" with her family in 1931, "We lived in a tent in the river bottom. We bought this tent from a widow whose husband had been disemboweled by a shovel handle when he had gone in to muck out after a blast that hadn't completely blown yet. ... We also had to get another tent. That tent was the one I cooked and we ate in. Then, we got another tent to sleep in. Between the tents, we spread blankets fastened to clothesline ropes with horse blanket pins so as to make a little shade for the children, because it was so hot down there. We bathed in the river. Of course, that meant that everybody had to wear some kind of apron or a little shift or something, and bathe the best they could. They dug some wells a little ways back from the river, but I saw that dirty looking utensils were being dipped into the wells until I was afraid to use the water. Of course, people had to use their utensils on campfires to cook. I told my husband that I just couldn't see drinking the water out of the wells. The water from the river, although it was pure, was so full of silt that you'd have to leave it to settle before you could drink it. He would get water from the mess halls for the road crew camp."

Chapter 3: Canyon Work

"Year in, year out, Crowe and Young and their 200-odd inspectors and foremen and their labor gang battle the Colorado twenty-four hours a day. The day shift comes on at 7:00 A. M. and knocks off at 3:00 P. M. Swing shift from 3:00 P. M. to 11:00 P. M. Graveyard from 11:00 P. M. to 7:00 A. M. The inevitably ribald slang of the construction camp has coined for the wives of the night workers the name of 'Graveyard Widows.' At night Black Canyon is lighted like a theatre with incredible clusters of sun arcs, bought from a bankrupt San Francisco ball park. The men come to work in covered lorries wearing papier-mache safety helmets that look like A. E. F. tin hats [The American Expeditionary Force was the force deployed to Europe in World War I]. These serve to protect them from falling rock--the greatest danger of the canyon work. Despite this precaution, in addition to a doctor and a field hospital at the base of the dam, over fifty men had given their lives to Boulder Dam by midsummer last year [1932]." – Excerpt from a 1933 article in *Fortune*

General Superintendent Frank Crowe (right) and Bureau of Reclamation Engineer Walter Young at the site

John Cahlan, one of the men who worked on the project, was quick to note "that before they could start the actual construction of Boulder Dam, there were two other major contracts that had to be completed. One was the road from Boulder City to the dam site; and the second was a railroad line from the Union Pacific Railroad out to Boulder City. That is the spur line that took off the Union Pacific main line about ten miles south of Las Vegas and went out to Boulder City. The railroad line is still in service, and the Union Pacific is servicing Henderson with that Boulder City line. At that time, there was no paved highway between Las Vegas and Boulder City. It was a dirt road and was nothing more than just a place cleared out, between here and Boulder City, so the cars could drive, if necessary. As they drove, ruts were dug into the dirt, about a foot or a foot and a half deep. You got your tires in the ruts, and that's where you had to stay. If somebody came along in the other direction, it was a major project to get one of the automobiles out of the rut so that the other one could pass it. But in 1932 the highway department put in a two-lane paved road which generally follows the same road that is there today."

In addition to working on the necessary transportation, the first step toward actually building the dam was to dig a number of large tunnels to divert the water of the Colorado River around the area where the dam would be built. According to Wilbur, "These diversion tunnels will be four in number, each 50 feet in diameter. Because of their size, their excavation will be very much like the operation of a quarry. The greatest problem will be the disposal of the excavated material. Part of it will be needed to build the cofferdams that will be placed in the river, above and below the site of the dam, to keep the water out of the excavation where the foundation of the dam is to be placed. The building of the road, the railroad, the tunnels, and the coffer dams will all precede the beginning of the great wedge, over 700 feet high, that is to close this river. While these earlier works are being built the final detailed plans for the dam will be completed."

Though he tried to explain the project in layman's terms, the Wilbur was aware that neither he nor most of his constituents would ever be able to fully grasp the planning and scientific calculations that went into the project. In fact, he once said, "Only engineers who have had considerable familiarity with dams and power development can fully appreciate all that is involved in these plans. The dam is not merely a mass of concrete to hold the water back. It is a complex industrial structure traversed by pipes and corridors, in which will be placed the regulating gates and the valves for the dynamos which will generate a million horsepower of electrical energy and the waste ways for controlling floods."

A picture of people touring the Hoover Dam's generators

A picture of a penstock used to transfer water to the Hoover Dam's turbines

A picture of some of the Hoover Dam's turbines

Another author focused on the sheer magnitude of the structure, a size that would ensure it a place on the list of history's greatest man-made marvels. He described it as "a concrete-arch, gravity-type dam which will tower 730 feet from canyon bedrock--almost as high as the…Woolworth Building. The base width will equal two city blocks. It will measure not much less than a quarter-mile across the top. The concrete used would build a standard sixteen-foot highway from Pensacola to Seattle--if you can visualize that. When complete it will back up the largest artificial body of water in the world, sufficient to cover Connecticut to a depth of ten feet. This will form a grimly beautiful lake 115 miles long and full of tourist steamboats."

According to an investigation by *Fortune* magazine, "Boulder Dam has four purposes," with the first one being "flood control." As the author reminded readers, the river it was damming up, while mighty and beautiful, also had a reputation for being treacherous to the surrounding area. The article explained, "The yellow Colorado water has for many years watered the rich desert farms of southern California and western Arizona. Often it flooded them, sweeping away budding crops, farmers' fords, and the farmers themselves. Boulder Dam will not only block the largest flood on record but it will hold almost two full years' flow behind its bulk, releasing a normal stream throughout the year. A sub-purpose is silt removal, whereby the muddy content will precipitate above the dam, simplifying and cheapening distribution to irrigation lands. Flood and silt have cost Southwest ranchers an estimated $2,000,000 yearly. This bill will have been paid for the last time when the Colorado, for the first time in thousands of years, flows evenly and clear to the Gulf."

In spite of the promise that the river would be safe, many preferred it untamed and in its natural state. Photographer W. A. Davis later complained, "I loved that old river. It was beautiful. I'd swam the river, I'd boated the river, I'd taken people up the river on trips…I felt bad to see it tamed, to tell you the truth."

The second purpose of the dam was "water conservation," since, according to the author writing in 1933, "Below the dam the Colorado now irrigates 660,000 acres of land. This acreage is limited by the low water flow. By storing spring floods, from five to seven times as much water will be available in summer, permitting irrigation on about 1,500,000 acres of new land 2,160.000 acres in all." As Blaine Hamann of the U.S. Bureau of Reclamation pointed out, "The river was an enemy, and only in short periods of time could you look at it as a useful river. Most of the time it was something that would kill you or ruin your farm."

The dam's third purpose was to supply water for "The Metropolitan Water District, comprising many cities and towns in southern California - principally Los Angeles." In fact, by 1933, those cities had already "contracted to take about a billion gallons daily from the river to wash southern California faces and water southern California lawns." According to one article, the "$220,000,000 aqueduct…will pay the U. S. about $250,000 yearly."

The final and most perhaps most obvious purpose of the dam was to supply electricity. As the author pointed out, "Under the mighty shadow of the dam will be built the biggest power plant in the world. This will develop 1,800,000 horsepower four times Niagara's power, thrice the ultimate capacity of Muscle Shoals. Already the electricity has been sold on fifty-year contracts to the city of Los Angeles and the Southern California Edison Co., which in turn subcontract 79 per cent of it (on percentages fixed by law) to Arizona, Nevada, the Metropolitan Water District, and smaller California valley towns."

Of course, the dam would cost people much more than money, as Wilbur pointed out when he said, "The greater part of the 150,000 acres which will be flooded is public land, but scattered through it are small areas of privately owned land, the largest one being in the valley of the

Virgin River." Though the population was scarce around the Boulder area at that time, many farmers and ranchers had to be uprooted from their home.

Naturally, nobody would ever fully understand the dam like the men who worked on it. One of them described some of the necessary tasks: "Now, a mucker was the one that had to clean the rock surface before the concrete was poured. This had to be clean enough so that you could practically eat off of it. Well, we did this for a while, and then I got a little better job: we went to concrete puddling. This is where you wore hip boots, you know, and a hard hat. They'd pour the concrete, and it was up to you to get it spread out with your feet. You had to work it pretty good, or you'd leave rock pockets. And you didn't dare do these because if you did, they had to be taken out and the space filled. This was hard work, you know. I was back in the various tunnels all this time, and they finally started pulling the plug, I think, in the number 2 tunnel on the Arizona side. At that time they put a monorail across the top of the main tunnel; then they could bring agitators full of concrete down on the main high line and set them on trucks. The trucks would back into this monorail, and there they would be picked up. I would hook them up and unhook them, just as a hook tender, and they would be monorailed back to where they needed the concrete."

After working on the tunnels for a awhile, that same worker admitted, "Well, of course, I still wanted a better job. So I asked Virginia Steelworkers, which at the time was tying all this reinforcing steel that went into all the walls of the various sections of the power house. And I got a job working for Herb Merner, who was the superintendent." This proved to be a good move, as he later recalled, "And so I tied steel. I went from...when I first went down there to the site as a laborer it was $4 a day, and then hook tender was $4.50 a day. Then I went to the steel crew at $5 a day. I finally got $5.60 a day tying steel. Well, when they finished pouring the plugs, and they started putting the penstocks in, too, why, it was up to the steelworkers to get the steel into these cradles that held the penstocks in place. All the steel was laid on top of the power house, and it was up to 2 or 3 of us to get ahold of one of these...oh, about 30-foot pieces of inch-and-a-quarter steel in a semicircle and get it through a small tunnel back to where they were used. Well, the journeymen $6-a-day men and the other $5.60-a-day men, myself included, were all doing the same work. So I asked Herb; I says, 'I want a raise. I want to get the same money they're getting.' He said, 'Young man, I'll pay a man for what they know, not for being you.' And so I worked on and kept pouring."

Chapter 4: Young and Crowe

A picture of ongoing construction

A picture of workers working on the power plants

"There are two reasons why Young and Crowe are not bitter enemies. One is that the job is too big for petty human friction. Young's inspectors and Crowe's foremen know this as well as their bosses. They know that friction which slows work quietly rubs somebody out of a job. The second reason is the mutual respect of Young and Crowe. Crowe spent years in the U.S. Reclamation Service, which Young now represents. He knows Young's duties and responsibility as well as Young does. 'I'd go to hell for him,' says Crowe. Frank Crowe, according to close guessers at the dam, gets $25,000 a year plus bonuses. Young gets $6,375. And this government work rates no bonus, there being no American Legion of the Reclamation Service. But regardless of salary, Walker Rollo Young is the boss at Boulder Dam. The U.S. hired the Six Companies, who hired Crowe. The U.S. flag flies just outside Young's office window." – Excerpt from a 1933 article in *Fortune*

One historian has called Frank Crowe the Six Companies' "ace in the hole." According to one article written in the early months of the dam's development, "Walker Young helped design the dam and is on hand to see that it rises exactly according to specifications. But the man who is actually building it, probably the best man for the job in the world, is Frank T. Crowe. He has been called the Colonel Goethals of Boulder Dam. ... Frank Crowe ... twists around in a chair a lot while he talks, preferring the outdoors, and makes an absolute rule that no letter shall go out of his office over one page long. He believes any idea can be expressed in that space and that anything longer is a waste of words. He had one dominant desire in life--to work on dams--and has gratified that desire almost steadily since Arrowrock. He was U.S. Construction Engineer on the Tieton Dam in Washington and General Superintendent of the Jackson Lake Dam in Wyoming. For private contractors he built the Guernsey Dam on North Platte and Combre Dam on Bear River, California. His last job was the Deadwood Dam in Idaho, which began by walking with his construction gang through seventy miles of snow."

Crowe was the General Superintendent hired to see to it that the dam got built as quickly and efficiently as possible. A man who preferred to see his hands smeared with mud rather than ink, he lived by the motto "Never my belly to a desk." A graduate of the University of Maine, he had worked for the Reclamation service for most of his life when he learned that a number of dams in the west were to be built by private contractors. Unwilling to miss out on the fun, he gave up his position with the Reclamation Service and went to work for a private company. When he heard about the Hoover Dam project, he recalled, "I was wild to build this dam. I had spent my life in the river bottoms, and (Hoover) meant a wonderful climax—the biggest dam ever built by anyone, anywhere."

Given that background, the Six Companies looked over his resume and the man himself and put him in charge. According to the same article, "He has one hobby-the development of men; specifically, the men who follow him by hundreds to work on his dams His principal exhibit is Bernard (Woody) Williams, who first worked for him at thirteen, and now, at thirty, is in complete charge when Crowe leaves Black Canyon for Boulder City. For Williams and his foremen he has only one working rule: 'To hell with excuses–get results!' He is tall, talks loudly, and laughs hard. He is noted for his humor. ... He knows thousands of construction laborers by their first names and 'generally how many kids they got.' ... He is down in Black Canyon most of the day and often part of the night. ... He conveys an irresistible impression of drive, and translates it into almost magical results. The men dislike to work that hard, but they like Crowe. They work that hard."

Elton Garrett, one of the men who worked for him, agreed with that description's sentiments: "Frank Crowe was a genius for organized thinking and for imparting organized thinking to other people... He not only was an engineering genius, he was a people genius. That went a long ways." Another worker, Red Wixson, later remembered, "He didn't want to listen to what was going on down there. He wanted to see it with his own eyes. I never saw him get excited about anything. If something went wrong, he was there to get an eye on it, to explain what was wrong, fix it. He was there to help you, not to fire you. One thing he knew was men. ... He respected his men. He was appreciative."

In spite of his good relationship with his men, Crowe was no pushover, which became apparent when the workers went out on strike in August 1931. According to Leo Dunbar, "[W]hen the Wobblies [Industrial Workers of the World] got in here and tried to get a strike going, there was plenty of trouble. Mr. [Sims] Ely [the Boulder City manager] was very strict about those things. He had a good set of rangers who took care of the job and did the work. Of course, that was one reason that the government decided to move everybody out who wasn't employed at that time." The workers felt that they were not being paid enough for the dangerous and unpleasant work they were being called upon to do, but Crowe felt they were being unreasonable and declared, "The workers will have to work under our conditions, or not at all." In a nation with double digit unemployment, he had the clout to make this stick, and the strike ended in a week.

For all that the dam was being built by private contractors, it was still a government project, and the other man wielding power in the project was Walter Young of the Reclamation Bureau. According to Crowe, he and Young "like to cry at each other and raise hell. He says my foremen are no good, but he don't mean anything." When asked about this, Young agreed, saying, "Yes, sometimes we fight with each other for the fun of it."

One article described Young's background: "The engineering career of this quiet, sharp-eyed man who at forty-eight is commander of the government guard at Boulder Dam began at the University of Idaho. He studied mining, in addition to working most of his way through, captaining the basketball team, and presiding over the student body. He…took a government job as a designer on the construction of Idaho's Arrowrock Dam, the Boulder Dam of its time. On this job he met Frank Crowe, bossing a shift for the head engineer. From that day to this he has worked in the Reclamation Service as field investigator, designer, administrator. He has figured hydraulics on more dams than he call remember, twenty five of them on the Colorado alone-- ghost dams which never rose from mounds of paper. He contributed materially to the first and basic designs for Boulder Dam. He wears glasses, and hasn't smoked for months. … He regards engineering as an art--"The Art of Economical Construction." Combined with his great talents both as a designer and administrator is his ability to make big decisions and small ones with equal speed."

According to the article, Young also played a crucial part in the strike: "When the fearful heat of the first summer at Boulder and the lack of proper accommodations combined to brew a riot, he met it by ordering everybody off the U. S. Reservation. Then he invited every man who wanted to work to come back, assuring him of the best possible living conditions in the shortest possible time. The men came back. Of course, what they came back to was another matter, and while the housing might have been improved, their dangerous job was made more so by the rush to complete the project ahead of schedule.

In addition to Young and Crowe, there were a number of other men leading the project. As Wilbur pointed out, "The Reclamation Bureau will have the cooperation of the engineers of the

Los Angeles Water and Power Department and the Southern California Edison Co. and its related companies. ... Its chief designing engineer, J. L. Savage, is recognized as a genius in his line. He has successively designed three dams which at the time of their construction were the highest in the world. ...In addition to the corps of experts on the permanent staff of the bureau, it has as consulting engineers, A. J. Wiley, who has an international reputation and is consulting engineer for the irrigation department of India; L. C. Hill, the designer and resident engineer on the Roosevelt Dam and many monumental works in this and other countries; and D. C. Henny, one of the foremost consulting engineers of the country. Because of the exceptional size of the dam and the difficult engineering problems involved, Congress thought it prudent to create a board of five — three engineers and two geologists — who would review the plans and estimates prepared by the Bureau of Reclamation and report direct to the President. The engineers on this board — Gen. Wm. L. Seibert, builder of Gatun Locks at Panama, Darnel W. Mead, and Robert Ridgway — have approved all of the work thus far sub mitted to them, and will pass judgment on the detailed plans of the dam when these have been completed."

Chapter 5: The Boulder Dam Worker

Pictures of workers

"The Boulder Dam worker of 1933 is a national type of some importance. He is a tough itinerant American--the 'construction stiff.' His average age is thirty-three. His average wage is sixty-eight cents an hour. He is taller and heavier than the average U. S. soldier, runs a greater risk of losing his life, and has passed a more drastic physical examination. He has been in most of the states of the Union and can find his Way in a dozen different kinds of unskilled and semi-skilled labor--a hoist in a Pennsylvania coal mine, a saw in Oregon, a shovel on a dozen road jobs. He has boiled a string of mules in Bluejacket, Oklahoma - followed a pipe line as it crept across a prairie, a few yards a day, toward a town invisible behind a hill range. He is inured to ceaseless, frightful heat--and fearful cold, too, for that matter. Four or five of him in an old car can always get to a row of lights on Saturday night and if some four-flusher cops his roll or his girl it may be a fight or a laugh-what's the difference?" – Excerpt from a 1933 article in *Fortune*

By 1933, the work on the dam was well underway, and thousands of people had pulled up stakes and moved to the desert in search of a job. Leo Dunbar was one of the married men who came to Boulder City with their families, and he remembered, "My wife and I had 3 small children.... The government had shipped my furnishings and everything we had down, and it was deposited in a brick house on Denver Street that had just been finished. Now, the plaster was wet, and everything was soaking, and, of course, they put the bedding on the floor in the living room and all the rest of the furniture on top of the bedding. I had been living in the camp on the site of what is now Lakeview. And after the family came down, some of the boys from the camp said, "Well, we'll help you get going." There was no heat in the house; we couldn't use electricity for heat, but there was an electric range that had just been installed. ... The next thing was to make ourselves beds. So what we did was we lighted the range and used the oven in the range, went out and found a bunch of big rocks, put them in the range and warmed them. And we wrapped them up in papers and put them in the beds at night. And that was my hardship in coming here. But I was lucky to have a job, and my work went on from there."

For many people from other parts of the country, the environment itself was the most difficult thing to get used to. After all, Hoover Dam was built in the middle of a desert, and the area was chosen in part because it was so unpopulated, due to the fact few people wanted to live there. Marion Allen, one of the workers, recalled, "This little house down there on Seventh Street, what the wife kicked about, the sand come in off the desert, and the floor would get about a half inch deep of sand, you know. She'd sweep it out; by the time she got it swept out, it would move back in. ... We lived there in that house pretty near 4 years. Rent was enormous; it was $15 a month. I think we paid $2 a month for water, but there was a restriction on that water- -you didn't water a yard, not even a green plant out there. If you did that, they'd be right down and they'd give you trouble and charge you double, which would be about $4, which wouldn't have been bad, but the second time, that was it. But they didn't kick about you running the water all night on the roof. And that was our cooling system. We'd fix the hose so it'd spray the roof and run down over the burlap canvas. That made our cooling. So that worked out pretty good. Otherwise, the worst thing we had to contend with was the heat- -trying to sleep. About the time you'd cool off a little- -about 6:00, 6:30 or 7:00 in the morning -- you had to be on the bus going to work. So as far as I was concerned, that was the hardest part of it. Otherwise, we were probably some of the fortunate ones. The other people that lived in the camps in tents and all- -who didn't have any refrigeration and very little water- -probably suffered a lot more."

Most of the families coming to Boulder had no idea how to cope with the living conditions there. Erma Godbey told of one particularly disturbing event: "Then I just got a terrible, terrible burn. My face was sunburned; it was windburned; it was campfire burned - - all 3. And I thought I'd caught some kind of a disease in the river. I was so afraid my children might get it that I . . . anybody that went into Vegas, I'd have them get me some Listerine and some cotton. And I was taking this pure Listerine and this cotton and dabbing my face, so I was drying it out and burning it with the Listerine as well as what was already there. It was just getting so terrible, I said to my husband, 'I've got to go to a doctor and see what's the matter with my face.' And he would laugh at me, because when I would change expression, I'd get little cracks, and they'd bleed. ... So, we made the trip to Las Vegas, and needless to say, there wasn't any highway. It was just up hills and down dale and in the arroyos and stuff and dust...the minute I opened the door and went into the doctor's office, he took one look at me, and he said, 'My God, woman! You've got the worst case of desert sunburn and windburn I've ever seen in my life!' ... Men used to go without a shirt, and then they would get such blisters on their back that sometimes they would be festered. And babies, especially - - people thought that they'd be cooler if they run around without anything, and they'd get these terrible sun blisters, and then they would open, and they would be infected."

Ironically, the housing project for the workers was built on a reservation formerly set aside by the government for use by Native Americans. It was also a highly controlled environment, as described by one author: "The gang on the job varies with the various steps in the dam's progress. The maximum estimated, but never reached, was 4,000 ... They eat and sleep in Boulder City, built on a U.S. reservation. Nobody call build houses or sell so much as a radish without a U.S. permit. And 80 per cent of the workers must live on the reservation."

This housing situation was made all the more ironic by the fact that the Hoover Dam was designed to help create the modern American West. The power it produced would allow a little town called Los Angeles to become one of the biggest cities in the world, and the men who built it would see another little town grow into a full-fledged tourist destination that had a seedy reputation even back then. As *Fortune* pointed out, "Las Vegas is a Nevada town twenty-three miles away, where drinking, gambling, and all the grosser forms of self-expression flourish."

Getting the men from their homes to the dam was a primary concern, and to accomplish this in the most organized way possible, the builders brought in large buses known as "transports." According to Mary Ann Merrill, whose husband worked on the dam, "They had a 2 decker, and they had different sized transports. They transported them all down there. [They would gather] up about Arizona Street and the Nevada Highway, because it seems to me I remember them getting off up there...where the bus came in, probably. But they had dormitories and the mess hall. Anderson had that on the west end of town, and they probably took the buses from there also. ... They just took them down there. Some of them went on down below; some of them on top, of course, according to where you were working on the dam."

Not surprisingly, working conditions were terrible. Godbey recalled, "The men would go to work, and so many of the men were passing out with heat stroke that they decided that they would go to work at 4:00 in the morning and work until noon. Nobody worked from noon until 4:00 p.m. because that was the heat of the day. Another crew come on at 4:00 and worked till midnight with searchlights. At that time they didn't know anything about taking extra salt, and people were sweating out all the salt in their bloodstream, and they were passing out. ... Now, this was the Depression, and so many men had walked miles and miles, and they had been without food also. So we had to go into Las Vegas. But you couldn't go into Las Vegas until you set a car in the river for 3 days. All the cars had wooden spokes in those days, and the spokes dried out so bad that they just rattled and came loose. So if you were going to go to Las Vegas, you had to set your car in the river, and then you had to move it a little bit - - not enough so as it'd float down the river, but enough so as the spokes would soak up - - before you could go into Las Vegas."

Over time, Boulder City grew and became more and more "civilized," but it was up to the residents to make many of the improvements they wanted to see. One woman explained, "At first, we didn't have any schools. There was no schools in Boulder at all, and so older kids had to go to Las Vegas to school, if they could get in there. Then they used 3 of the first Six Company houses built- -they were down fairly close to the El Rancho Motel, down in there- -and they used those for school buildings. Different women here in town who had taught school before they had come to Boulder City volunteered to teach. And people would pay a dollar and a half- -I don't know whether it was a week or a month- -per child. (I think it was a month.) And if they had 2 children, why, the second child was a dollar. There were no books or anything. They just had to do the best they could. Then, of course, we all raised cain because we didn't have any school. But this was a reservation; it wasn't a part of the state of Nevada. And so then we did get started to build a school. The first school was a brick building, which is now our city hall, and it didn't get finished until the latter part of September of 1932. The Six Companies contacted the school district in Las Vegas, and they told them what books they would need, and they kept them in their store. The people had to buy books for the children, and the school just didn't have any equipment at all. They had to do so much using the gelatin and making papers from the books for the kids to study from because there was never enough books in the Six Companies Store for the people even to buy when they could buy. It was about 3 years later when the state bought the books back from us. But, at first, the government built the building, and Six Companies hired the teachers. But we did go by the curriculum of the state of Nevada."

Chapter 6: Thinking in Giant Terms

"Accustomed to thinking in giant terms they are not particularly moved because the dam has been given a new label by the Roosevelt Administration. The reversion of the name from Hoover Dam to Boulder Dam is considered around Black Canyon as politics. It is unofficially estimated that the shift may cost the U.S. some $200,000 in printing bills to change the staggering mass of documentary record that a dam entails. But that is no concern of the builders. Their world is bounded by the desert mountains and their lives are for the current years dedicated to a job." – Excerpt from a 1933 article in *Fortune*

In 1933, the new Secretary of the Interior, a Roosevelt appointee named Harold Ickes, issued an announcement that the Hoover Dam would become officially known as the Boulder Dam. While he did not admit this publicly, Ickes held a grudge against Hoover, the man his boss had recently defeated for president. Congressman Jack Anderson later commented, "I visited the Hoover Dam in 1933 and went all through it just about the time it was ready for completion and just before they turned the water into the penstocks. I always felt when Roosevelt and Ickes took down the plaque which dedicated the dam to Hoover--to whom it was originally dedicated--that a great injustice had been done to a great American, so I bided my time, hoping that the opportunity would arise when I could rectify what I considered a gross error. Well, in the 80th Congress, as you know -- that's the only Congress in which the Republicans controlled the House and the Senate out of the fourteen years that I served -- I decided it was time to introduce a bill to restore the name 'Hoover' to the then Boulder Dam." Anderson succeeded, and the name was changed back in 1947.

Ickes

Of course, the name meant little to those working on the project itself; they were far more preoccupied with staying on schedule. The government's contract with the Six Companies stated that the diversion tunnels had to be completed and the river moved by the end of October 1934 or the companies would be fined. As worker Tommy Nelson remembered, "The Six Companies foremen, they were on me all the time. Keep the trucks movin', everybody movin'. I was the flagman, flaggin' dump trucks. And lo and behold I took a look up, and saw a high scaler way up high on the Nevada side comin' down, and he fell very close to where I was standing. So I take a quick look, thinking that there's no trucks coming, and make a mad dash over to this guy. There's nothin' I can do for him. Along comes a hard-boiled superintendent, and I told him there's a man killed over there. And he said to me, in no uncertain terms, 'What are you going to do with all these blankety-blank trucks? Eat 'em? Get the trucks moving! He can't hurt anybody.'"

Completed tunnel lining at intake portal of diversion tunnel No. 4, looking toward entrance. Pressure for grouting jumbo seen in operation.

By May 1932, the tunnels to divert the mighty Colorado River were complete, thanks in large part to a giant device known as a drilling jumbo, which consisted of three levels of drills mounted on a 10 ton truck. When it was time to dig, the men carefully backed the truck up to the wall they were blasting and used the 30 drills to drive holes into the rock. They then placed dynamite in the completed holes and drove the drilling jumbo away to the next area. W. A. Davis explained, "That was a pretty clever idea. Because before, they'd have to put up staging. Then the staging would have to be taken down when they blew the face. And then they'd have to replace it. It was a big time saver." When Wilbur asked him how smooth the tunnels were,

Crowe proudly boasted, "As smooth as a schoolmarm's leg, Mr. Wilbur, and if I remember my geography that's pretty smooth."

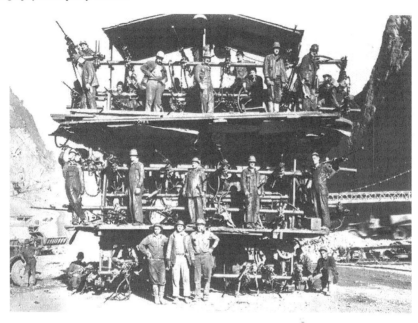

Workers on a drilling jumbo used to drill the tunnels

Of course, the drilling jumbo was hardly the only piece of specialized equipment used to build the dam. According to one author writing in 1933, "The biggest trucks in the world had to be designed and built by Mack. Powered with 250-horsepower motors and equipped with special duralumin bodies, they are capable of waddling away with sixteen cubic yards of earth–just twice the capacity of the biggest truck hitherto. Babcock & Wilcox of Barberton, Ohio, is building $10,908,000 worth of piping at a special plant erected one mile from the dam site. A General Electric unit will X-ray every inch of welding in the two and eight-tenths miles of penstocks (giant pipes carrying water from dam to power house). This world's record X-ray job involves 159,000 separate pictures and 24,000,000 square inches of film-a prodigious guaranty of welding quality. The government cableway which spans the abyss has five times the capacity of any earlier cableway. Built by Ledgerwood Manufacturing Co. of Elizabeth, New Jersey, it has six steel ropes bigger than the average man's wrist (three and one-half inches diameter) and can lower 150 tons of concrete or steel hundreds of feet from the upper workings to the pit. Engineers say it could take 200 tons or more. The roller cradle which runs along the cable dangling these crushing weights is as big as a box car. The turbines and generators for the power plant are also the largest to date: four of the turbines, contracted for by Allis-Chalmers, will turn up 115,000 horsepower apiece. The fifty-foot diversion tunnels dwarf New York's subway tubes. Fantastic machines called Jumbos run on rails into these tunnels. One has thirty-two air drills to perforate the rock; another has seven platforms, like the carriages on a ferris wheel, and carries the men who trim the walls after the rock has been blasted out; another lines the walls with. concrete--an eighty-foot section at a stop."

Even after the tunnels were completed, however, it took another year of backbreaking work to actually change the river's course from its accustomed banks to the concrete and steel tunnels. On April 23, 1933, reporters and photographers came from around the country to witness the great event. According to Nelson, "At 11:30 in the morning, a blast was put off down there, near the entry, in one of the big diversion tunnels. That was what put the show on the road." One historian explained, "Throughout the day, workers furiously dumped tons of rock into the river's path, trying to build a barrier high enough and strong enough to push it back into the tunnels. By dawn, the battle was won. Man had moved the mighty Colorado from the bed it had known for 12 million years. For Frank Crowe, it was a personal triumph — he had beaten the river, and his deadline, by eleven months." Ila Clements-Davey recalled, "The men were just swarming over the whole place, they just looked like a hill of ants they really did. It was just fantastic to watch all that going on. It was a monumental task."

Once the river was out of the way, the work began to go very quickly. The high-scalers went to work, dangling from ropes 800 feet above the ground and drilling into the sides of the canyon left behind with jackhammers, all while also using dynamite to blast out bigger chunks of rock. Clements-Davey described the scene: "It was like a movie of Tarzan, you know. You'd hear the blast and then see those guys fling themselves down there and start ripping the rocks off and there were people above them and people below them." Likewise, Maxine Riepen, who worked as a secretary for the company, said, "I remember this big, strong-looking man fell. And, uh, he yelled as he fell and this high-scaler below him swung out and caught him as he was falling and saved his life. Oh, he got write-ups and was quite a hero after that. Others... there were two or three that fell to their death. Maybe even more."

Pictures of "high-scalers" drilling into the canyon high above the river

Time was money, and by the end of 1933, the Six Companies were ahead by two years and $3 million, but under Ickes, the Six Companies were forced to integrate their formerly all-white force, and eventually, black workers came to make up a significant percentage of the 4,000 men working on the project at any given time. However, even Ickes was not about to insist that these men be allowed to move their families into Boulder City. As Clements-Davey put it, "This was a closed community. Negroes were not, there was no way a Negro could get in here. No way anyone with a colored skin could get in here."

June 6, 1933 was a monumental day as the first bucket of concrete was poured into the canyon. By this time, there were 5,000 men working on the project, all supervised by Crowe, and under his direction, multiple cables were strung up around the site to carry concrete from place to place. When working at capacity, these cables could deliver a 20 ton bucket of concrete where it was needed every 78 seconds.

Of course, this was incredibly dangerous work, and one worker, John Cahlan, told a story about it with the callousness of a man who had seen too much suffering: "[One man] was riding a -- they had these big cableways across the top of the canyon that were used to lower and raise the buckets of cement that went down. The cement plants were up on top of the canyon, and they would lower the batches of cement down by these huge buckets. They were on a big hook, and they'd just lower 'em right down from the top of the canyon. And the guys used to ride these -- ride the hook up and down and pay no attention to it. It's just like construction on some of these skyscrapers. They never think anything of riding those hooks. This fellow was on with a big bucket of cement. They were about -- oh, they just started in to drop when the hook broke. As he was going down, he waved to the boys goodbye, and they dug him out of about four or five feet of dirt. He hit down at the bottom of the canyon, and just dug a big hole in there. They finally got him, but he, as I say, he never wavered for a moment. He was just wavin' the boys goodbye!"

Pictures of the dam's columns being gradually filled with concrete

Anyone who has seen photos of the dam notices that it is not one solid wall of concrete. Had the builders tried to pour such a wall, it would still be dry today over 75 years later. Instead, they created 5 foot tall blocks that were then stacked together in an interlocking pattern until they reached the top of the dam. Under Crowe's careful direction, and with his enthusiastic support, the crew poured the last bucket of concrete needed to complete the 72 story-tall dam on February 6, 1935. By the time it was complete, the Hoover Dam was over 720 feet tall, over 1,200 feet long, and over 650 feet wide at its base.

Chapter 7: The Dam's Legacies

A memorial at the site commemorating those who died working on the Hoover Dam

"It is in these matters of personnel, organization, and efficiency rather than in miracles of machinery that Boulder Dam is unique in engineering history. No problems have arisen which have not been solved before on other dams. The machines differ from previous ones principally in their gigantic size. ... Many of the tools in Black Canyon are on a similar scale, too big and too complicated for the layman to grasp without extensive comparative pictures and diagrams. But the engineers are modestly positive on one point: among the dam's legacies to the world will be numbered no new machine device. No puzzles of construction or design have faced them that have not been solved before. The major problem has been the job's brutal size." – Excerpt from a 1933 article in *Fortune*

Just a few days after the last concrete was poured, the gates on the diversion tunnel were closed and the mighty Colorado began to feed a new lake, Lake Mead, which quickly became the largest manmade reservoir on the planet. When full, it covered about 250 square miles and was 500 feet deep. Clements-Davey remembered, "We got into what I call now the little puddle that was the lake at that time, and we went up to the back part of the dam and this great big structure this, oh my God… big hunk of concrete, corkin' up the Colorado River. And the intake towers sitting on the cliffs, way up above us. Now when you go over the dam it looks like the intake towers are right in the middle of the lake, you know, and, and the dam, you only see a small portion of it. You can't get the feeling of the immensity of the dam, and it looks a lot bigger from that side then it does from the face side. It really does."

A picture of Lake Mead beginning to fill in against the Hoover Dam

Indeed, the look of the dam had always been a priority among its designers. According to an article which appeared in *Reclamation Era*, the magazine of the Reclamation Commission, "Probably the most significant and appropriate innovation is the selection of the decorative motifs and color scheme of our southwestern Indians as the basis of all decoration at the dam. These motifs or patterns and the distinctive color palette are eminently appropriate as well as beautifully adapted to the purpose. In the pottery designs, basketry patterns, and sand paintings of the Colorado River watershed there exists a wealth of wholly untouched and magnificent source of material….With aboriginal directness these forms are derived from stepped mesas, rain, lightning, and louds…from lizards, plumed serpents, and birds…and the fertility of invention with which these native forms and abstractions are assembled seems unlimited. The bold, frank appositions of form or color and the novelty of application or use give them a quality all their own. For character, style, and distinction there is nothing to compare with them, and their inherent boldness makes them peculiarly adaptable for use in connection with modern architecture."

The exterior of the dam was not the only area that received careful design and decoration. According to the article, "a design [is] to be executed in dull green and black terrazzo for the lobby floor of the elevator towers at the top of the dam. The walls of these lobbies are to be of highly polished black marble and the ceilings of the most modern…treated aluminum with concealed lighting. The doors are of verdigris bronze which accords with the note of green and somber shade which is dictated by the need for a cool effect when arriving in the lobbies from the blazing heat of the dam crest. The floor design itself is an adaptation of two Pima basket patterns adjusted in scale…to the requirements of the space and location. A little study of its central portion will reveal its striking similarity to what might be termed an engineer's basic diagram of a generator or turbine, with valves, gates, and a suggestion of centrifugal motion. What basic motif could be more appropriate or better adapted?"

September 30, 1935 was set aside as the date for the dam's dedication, and on that day, 20,000 people came to Nevada to see what a number of newspapers were already calling the 8th wonder of the world. President Roosevelt himself came to the dam to dedicate it, and in prepared remarks, he said:

"This morning I came, I saw and I was conquered, as everyone would be who sees for the first time this great feat of mankind.

We are here to celebrate the completion of the greatest dam in the world, rising 726 feet above the bedrock of the river and altering the geography of a whole region; we are here to see the creation of the largest artificial lake in the world— 115 miles long, holding enough water, for example, to cover the State of Connecticut to a depth of ten feet; and we are here to see nearing completion a power house which will contain the largest generators yet installed in this country.

All these dimensions are superlative. They represent and embody the accumulated engineering knowledge and experience of centuries; and when we behold them it is fitting that we pay tribute to the genius of their designers. We recognize also the energy, resourcefulness and zeal of the builders, who, under the greatest physical obstacles, have pushed this work forward to completion two years in advance of the contract requirements. But especially, we express our gratitude to the thousands of workers who gave brain and brawn to this great work of construction.

We know that, as an unregulated river, the Colorado added little of value to the region this dam serves. When in flood the river was a threatening torrent. In the dry months of the year it shrank to a trickling stream. The gates of these great diversion tunnels were closed here at Boulder Dam last February. In June a great flood came down the river. It came roaring down the canyons of the Colorado, through Grand Canyon, Iceberg and Boulder Canyons, but it was caught and safely held behind Boulder Dam.

Across the San Jacinto Mountains southwest of Boulder Dam, the cities of Southern California are constructing an aqueduct to cost $220,000,000, which they have raised, for the purpose of carrying the regulated waters of the Colorado River to the Pacific Coast 259 miles away.

Across the desert and mountains to the west and south run great electric transmission lines by which factory motors, street and household lights and irrigation pumps will be operated in Southern Arizona and California.

Boulder Dam and the powerhouses together cost a total of $108,000,000. The price of Boulder Dam during the depression years provided [work] for 4,000 men, most of them heads of families, and many thousands more were enabled to earn a livelihood through manufacture of materials and machinery.

And this picture is true on different scales in regard to the thousands of projects undertaken by the Federal Government, by the States and by the counties and municipalities in recent years.

Throughout our national history we have had a great program of public improvements, and in these past two years all that we have done has been to accelerate that program. We know, too, that the reason for this speeding up was the need of giving relief to several million men and women whose earning capacity had been destroyed by the complexities and lack of thought of the economic system of the past generation.

In a little over two years this great national work has accomplished much. We have helped mankind by the works themselves and, at the same time, we have created the necessary purchasing power to throw in the clutch to start the wheels of what we call private industry. Such expenditures on all of these works, great and small, flow out to many beneficiaries; they revive other and more remote industries and businesses. Labor makes wealth. The use of materials makes wealth. To employ workers and materials when private employment has failed is to translate into great national possessions the energy that otherwise would be wasted. Boulder Dam is a splendid symbol of that principle. The mighty waters of the Colorado were running unused to the sea. Today we translate them into a great national possession.

Today marks the official completion and dedication of Boulder Dam. This is an engineering victory of the first order—another great achievement of American resourcefulness, American skill and determination.

That is why I have the right once more to congratulate you who have built Boulder Dam and on behalf of the Nation to say to you, 'Well done.'"

While the men were officially finished with the dam, it was not finished with them. In an eerie coincidence worthy of *Ripley's Believe It or Not*, Patrick Tierney slipped and fell into an intake tower on December 20, 1935, and he drowned before he could be rescued, thereby becoming the final fatality in the dam's construction. What gave so many people shivers was that he died exactly 13 years to the day after his father, surveyor J.G. Tierney, had become the project's first casualty after drowning on site. As a result, of the over 100 people to die working on the Hoover Dam, father and son were the project's first and last fatalities.

A 1998 picture of the Hoover Dam releasing water from the jet-flow gates

A modern view of the Hoover Dam

Bibliography

Bureau of Reclamation (2006). *Reclamation: Managing Water in the West: Hoover Dam*. US Department of the Interior.

Dunar, Andrew J.; McBride, Dennis (2001) [1993]. *Building Hoover Dam: An Oral History of the Great Depression*. Reno, Nev.: University of Nevada Press.

Hiltzik, Michael A. (2010). *Colossus: Hoover Dam and the Making of the American Century*. New York: Free Press.

Stevens, Joseph E. (1988). *Hoover Dam: An American Adventure*. Norman, OK: University of Oklahoma Press.

The Story of the Hoover Dam. Las Vegas: Nevada Publications, Inc. 2006.

Printed in Great Britain
by Amazon